I AM *L*ANNIE

*The Inspiring Story of
Lannie Dennis*

I AM LANNIE
The Inspiring Story of Lannie Dennis

Published by
Kingdom Publishing, LLC
Odenton, MD

Printed in the U.S.A.

Copyright ©2019 by Lannie Dennis

All rights reserved. No part of this book may be reproduced, stored in retrieval system, or transmitted in any form or by any means - electronic, mechanical, photocopy, recording or otherwise - except for brief quotations in printed reviews, without the prior written permission of the author.

Unless otherwise indicated, all Scripture quotations are taken from the Holy Bible: New International Version® Copyright © 1973, 1978, 1984 by International Bible Society. Used by permission of Zondervan Publishing House. All rights reserved.

Photographs provided by the author.

Library of Congress Control Number: 2019912884

ISBN Paperback: 978-1-947741-51-5
ISBN eBook: 978-1-947741-52-2

DEDICATION

In memory of:

My father, Thomas M Dennis (Lannie), my grandfather, Thomas Ira Dennis, my great great grandfather, Josh Dennis, my brother James Nick, and my father and mother in-law, Freddie and Ruth Cook. Calvin Downs, a good friend of ours, a real encourager.

FOREWORD
by Bishop Antonio M. Palmer
Kingdom Celebration Center, Odenton, MD

Everyone will experience some form of hardship and difficulty at some point in life. It can be the loss of a loved one, a financial pitfall, a marriage gone south or unfair harsh treatment from others, etc.

I remember when my wife and I suffered the tragic loss of our son from the painful grip of suicide. How devastating of a blow life brought us. But it is stories like the Lannie Dennis story which you are about to read that gives inner strength and the mental fortitude to get up and keep fighting no matter what challenges life may throw at you.

There aren't too many people I know who can go through decades of battling physical discomfort like Lannie. Although he suffers daily, he fights a tenacious fight against multiple diseases and the emotional pressure that comes with it.

In this book you will discover the power of having faith in God, friends who can encourage you and family who will support you with unwavering love and loyalty.

I am so glad that I met Lannie, because God used him to teach me more about faith and strength than I could ever learn in a seminary class or reading a biblical commentary. He walks out his faith in plain sight for others to see how God's strength is made perfect in our weakness.

TABLE OF CONTENT

Introduction 6

My Childhood 7

Dairy Farm Living 11

Columbia Beach 21

Motorcycle Organization 27

Cancer 31

Blindness 55

Crohn's Disease 73

Faces of Valor 79

Notes From My Family 87

Helpful Scriptures 91

Thank You 97

Poem by My Son, Cory Dennis 101

Pictures 105

INTRODUCTION

This is really something! I always thought about writing a book, but never fathom that I could put into words how God brought me through my indescribable journey. Now, I am literally on my way to doing so, with the help and prayers of my family and closest of friends.

For those that are reading this book. Some things may sound graphic, but if I am going to tell the story, I have to tell it as vivid as I experienced going through it. Some of you already know, because you have been through it with me. I got such an overwhelming response from my Coffee Talk Videos that Bari put together. Some viewers said that I should tell my whole story to help someone, because the video only shows a portion. The video can be viewed on YouTube; if you wish, you can view it before you read the book: "Ringing the Bell, New Beginning."

MY CHILDHOOD

You may ask, "Who is Lannie Mayhew Dennis?" Well, let me tell you all about him as I take you on this journey. I am convinced that you may not put this book down until you're finished.

I was born June 3, 1950 at Johns Hopkins Hospital in Baltimore, Maryland. I am the son of Thomas M Dennis, whom we also called, Lannie and my mother is Carrie A Dennis. We lived in a very small rural town called, Shadyside, Maryland on a Dairy Farm. My father worked on the farm and my mother cleaned houses and cooked for various families. The farm belonged to Benet Crownell. We lived in the house that was on their farm. There was a downstairs and upstairs, two bedrooms a kitchen and living room were downstairs. There was no running water or bathroom in the house, but we were fortunate enough to have electricity.

As for our living arrangements, in one of the bedrooms downstairs, my mother and father slept in one bed, while me and my older sister, Shirley Ann (Holland) slept in the other bed in the same room. My older brother, James (Jimmy), was sleeping upstairs on one side of the attic, and my grandfather had the other side of the attic. My aunt, who we call, Doll Baby (Eliza Dennis), had the other bedroom downstairs.

We had a wood stove for heat and a gas stove for cooking. When I was very young, I used to like to play, "Cowboys." I remember the house being surrounded by a lot of woods. We had chickens and pigs – we even had a Billy-goat at one point in time – and a couple dogs. My dad always had a garden with potatoes, tomatoes, kale, string beans, and squash. He liked to go hunting for rabbits, squirrels, dove and coon. He would eat all those things. He also told me when I was old enough to hunt, "Do not shoot anything, unless you were going to eat it." One thing I liked about the farm was something I remember when I was about 6 or 7 years old. I was to go down to the farm and sit in my brother's or father's lap and drive the tractors. The reason why this was so dear to me is because my dad couldn't really go any place; his job was a 7-days a week kind of job, and the cows had to be milked twice a day. At times, by me being so young, I would go to work with my mother, because there was no one home to watch me. I liked when I got old enough to go down on the farm with my dad and my brother.

Also, at an early age, I had a big stuttering problem. I couldn't get my words out. I used to stomp my feet trying to get my words out. It was so frustrating! On top of that, I was teased and laughed at all the time. That is why today I do not laugh at anyone who stutters or have any issues. I think I developed a quick temper as a result of people laughing at me and I couldn't do anything about it at the time. So, I carried that with me until I got some help. I've gotten way better, but I'm still working on it a little today.

When my cousins, Walter, Willie, Sydney, Thomas and Quintin would stay

Dad with a horse

with us, they had to stay upstairs with my brother Jimmy, because we didn't have much room. Some of them would sleep on the couch. My aunt Doll Baby lived with us. Sometimes my uncle Quintin, Sr. would stay overnight. As I am writing this book, all of my aunts and uncles, except Elisa Dennis, have passed away. I am only writing what I can remember, so I may have missed some people. Like the church folk would say, "Charge to my head and not my heart." Somehow, we always had a lot to eat. I remember that on Sundays we had two or three different kinds of meat, and greens and vegetables. By the way, the preachers loved to come to our house on Sundays (smiles).

My Dad, Grandfather and Me when I was a little boy

DAIRY FARM LIVING

Let's talk about living on a Dairy Farm. I can remember when my father and brother would get up every morning at about 3:30am. They had to milk the cows about 4 or 5 o'clock. They had to walk about one half of a mile just to get to the barn. Then, they had to roundup the cows from out of the field to get them into the barn to milk them. I remember that they had a radio, but no one could reach it. It was always stuck on one station, WCAO. My brother hooked it up, where like a light switch, all we had to do was turn the radio on when we came into the barn. My brother was about six years older than me and two or three years older than my sister (something like that). Imagine, there was not even one bathroom on the farm.

Back to the cows; I think the barn held about

20 stalls for the cows to be milked. If I remember correctly, after they got one set of cows in, they would milk them first before bringing in another set of cows. My brother had to leave from milking the cows to going to school.

There was another building about two or three hundred feet from where they milked the cows. They took the milk to that building and poured it into a 5/600-gallon tank with a stir to keep it cold. It had a temperature gauge on it to monitor the coldness. That building was sterilized, but in the same building on the other side, there were two very large sinks to wash out the milking machines and clean everything, so that they would be clean for the next time you milked the cows. I liked going in that building, because there was heat and running water in there. Sometimes when I wanted to get away from everyone and the cows, I would sneak away into that particular building.

Now, when you finished milking cows in the morning, you had to clean the barn out and get the poop out. My father was doing that for years. On the farm they had a bull to keep the cows happy, so that the cows could have calves. That bull was mean; you couldn't even get close to him. But my father wasn't afraid of anything. He used to clean the bullpen out, too. In order to do so, he had to get the bull off into another pen, then, once he finished cleaning the bullpen, he had to get him back into his pen. He was fearless! But one time, the bull jammed my father between a fence and a pole. OUCH! Thank God my brother was there! I don't know what they did, but somehow my father got loose. He really could have been killed. My fearless father went right back the next day and continued to do the same thing. It never fazed my father.

As I am writing this, I remember more of the things that my father used to do. At that time, I didn't realize how blessed I was to be around him, to see and learn some things. Believe me, I was glad that I was there to work on the dairy farm for a while. I don't mind visiting one, but I would never work on one again. I take my hat off to those who work on them. Also, they have new technology now, but you still have to take the cows out and bring them in and get food for them.

I digress to say, I didn't realize that we were poor (money wise), but we weren't poor when it came to food and family fellowship. I didn't realize that at that time, but we were all together in one place.

Well, on the farm, you just didn't milk the cows and go home. If it was summertime you had to plant and grow hay, and bale it for the cows to eat. Also, you had to plant food and put in the siloes so that the cows had food for the winter. Then, you had to get ready to milk the cows again about 4 or 5 o'clock in the evenings. If you think about it, my father and brother would go to the farm about 5:00am, come home to get lunch about 12 or 1pm or they may have lunch with them (sometimes they had to eat while they were working). They wouldn't get home until about 7:00pm at night from work. If it was summertime, it was light outside longer. Sometimes when we finished milking the cows, we had to go out into the field to get hay for the cows to eat. So, sometimes you were out working until 7 or 8 at night.

    I can say this, I worked, but I never worked as hard as my father and brother worked on the farm, because I was too young. I would get the driving jobs, while they were throwing stuff on the trailer. So, when I was in the 5th or 6th grade I started going with my father and brother sometimes down to milk the cows before I went off to school. At this time, my brother was out of school and just working on the farm.

    Sometimes, I rode my bike to school. I didn't usually ride it through the barn, but this particular day I did before I went to school. I went home and changed clothes and went to school (I think I was in the 6th grade then). I rode my bike to school, putting it right beside the window where my classroom was at. The windows were up in the classroom. During class that morning, someone said, "What is that smell?" Then a couple of people began to repeat, "What's that smell?" I know I didn't have anything on me, because I had washed up and changed clothes. Then I remembered that, I had ridden through the barn, and I had cow poop on my tires and didn't know it. As I sat there, I realized where the smell was coming from, but I didn't say anything. I was waiting for our first break. We would get two breaks, one in the morning and the other in the evening. It was about 10 or 10:15am, we went out to play a little while. When we finally went outside, I moved my bike away from the window and moved it a distance away near some trees. We didn't have any more problems with the smell that day (smiles). I never rode my bike through the barn again while on my way to school.

    A couple of things I liked about the farm was that I had the chance to drive the tractors in the field; and sometimes onto the main road. I like the dogs and cats and having lots of animals around. As I look back now, I see that I learned a lot and wish I had paid a little more attention. I thank my father and brother for letting me come down to the barn to be with them while they worked. I know a lot of times I was probably in the way. But believe me, on a dairy farm, they can find something for anybody to do. It is a lot of work, seven days a week. Besides milking cows and tending to other animals, we sometimes had to cut wood, then sell it to whomever needed it. There was a lot of wood on the farm.

I remember my dad loved working on that farm and working in his garden. He loved all the animals, too. He especially loved giving away food from his garden. He would take food around the community and leave it on people's porches or at their front door – and this was to anyone; he didn't care if you were white or black. He was kindhearted and loved to share. One time, he was in the newspaper because of the baby deer he found in the woods. Its mother wasn't around or got killed or something. He put it in one of the buildings and nursed it back to health. Afterwards, he turned it loose on its own.

I remember my aunt Doll Baby (Elisa), when she was at Mr. Crownell's house. She used to work up at the house; she also prepared our lunches there. Most of the time, we went up to the house to eat lunch. We had some good times when our aunts and uncle would come visit us. Sometimes dad would take some of them down to the barn, because he still had to milk the cows (at least until he got off from work on Sunday). My mother made sure we went to church every Sunday. I don't think my brother went, because he had to go and help my dad during that time of morning.

I guess I didn't realize how much we loved each other until one of us got hurt or if someone else was messing with us. For some odd reason, we didn't say the word "love" in our home, but we knew we all loved each other; it just wasn't spoken. That was the way our parents were raised, and their parents were raised. You have to remember at this time we had to go into the back doors of buildings and stores. There weren't any integrated schools either. I even saw a cross after it was burned. It was burnt the night before. My father took me to see where it had been burned at a church. I remember they used to have carnivals down in Deale, but being black, you couldn't go down there. If you did, you went down at your own risk. So, I understand why our parents were so strict on us about going out and knowing our whereabouts at all times. They were just trying to keep us safe. I can't even begin to imagine what happened to them or what they may have seen during their time of growing up, until the time they showed me the burnt cross.

I recall when I was about 10 years old. I had one particular white friend (at least I thought he was my friend). He and his father used to come to our farm and talk to my father and Mr. Crownell for hours, and we played while they talked. They had a horse farm and my dad and I use to go there and play in the house. This went on for years and years. One day, while riding with my father in the truck and stopping for gas, I saw my friend standing next to the garage talking to another white guy that I knew (not as well as I knew my friend). When we pulled up to the gas pump, my dad also noticed my friend with the other white kid. I thought it quite strange when my dad got out of the truck, told me to stay inside the truck. I know my dad knew that was my buddy and that my dad had seen him. I know he knew how tight we were and how we played together all the time. My dad was talking to someone at the pump when he was getting his gas. I got out of the truck to see my friend, the one I played with for years. It was a regular garage where you work on cars and was well-known in the area. My friend was standing by the garage bay door on the outside. The garage door was up where he could hear me. So, I was grinning and calling his name. I know he should have heard me. I walked closer. I got so close I could reach out and touch him. He was facing the other guy and they were talking. I know he knew it was me, because he looked over at my dad and I at one time. I called him again, this time touching him while calling his name.

He finally acknowledged me, but I could feel something. It was the first time I had this feeling from someone who was supposed to be my friend. I felt that I wasn't wanted there, and he didn't want anyone to know that he knew me or that we were friends. By that time, my dad had called me and I got back in the truck. I told my father that so-and-so acted a little funny. He said I told you to stay in the truck anyway. I then understood why he had told me to do that. Every time I saw my friend, it was on the farm where we worked or at their farm. I had never seen him any place else. We left and went back to the house.

A couple of years after that, the Weems family took over the farm. Nothing changed, we still worked the farm. I can remember my mother saying that we needed our own house. She worked for enough people that could help her get the permit and stuff. We were able to have our house built. When we moved into our house, I was about 13 years old. Now, if you read the first part of this book, you know that the old house where we lived there was a lot of people and no bathrooms, just an outside toilet. We did have electric and we had a hand pump outside to pump water. So, when we moved into our new house, we had three bedrooms. My sister had her bedroom, my parents had their bedroom, and my brother and I had a bedroom and most of all, we had a bathroom inside the house with running water. I thought I had died and went to heaven. On the first night, I didn't know whether to sleep in my bedroom or in the bathroom.

Everything looked good. As I am writing this, my mother is still living in that house by herself at 96 years of age. Her birthday is September 7th, and she will be 97 years old.

In the summertime, around the time I was 13 years old, I started working with the Leatherbury well drilling company. It was way down in La Plata and Waldorf, Maryland. There, we did not have an electric drill, we had to turn it ourselves, using manual strength. It didn't have a motor – you were the motor. On top of that, in the summertime it was very hot and, in the winter, it was extremely cold. When I went to the job some winter mornings, and it had snowed, I remember the pipes being on the ground, and we had to get them up out of the snow. Our job required us to work outside even in the snow. I had about three or four layers of clothes on while working in those winter months. Sometimes, I had wished I was back down on the farm in the barn where the cows were.

COLUMBIA BEACH

I also met some new friends at Columbia Beach that were from Washington, DC. like Reginald and Bryan Travis, and Billy Minor. I met these guys through a mutual friend, Gilbert Nick. We all became friends; these guys used to race boats professionally. I used to go with Billy to some of the other boat races like the Ms. Budweiser race. In the summer, we would hang out down on the beach on the water. I think it was a place called Rooster Tail, somewhere a little way out from Calvert County. These guys used to get together with the people that owned Rooster Tail and get the boats ready for racing. If I remember correctly, the Bruster Tail used to meet other places with Billy and them, and they would put their boats in the water.

One time, however, the guys wanted us to meet at their place. It was on a Sunday - that I remember well. When we got to Rooster Tail the boat place, they told us to go ahead and meet them at the boat ramp down the street. They would be along about 20 minutes. We had about six cars that were pulling racing boats behind them. It was an older guy with us that was in charge who had the directions. We were told to go down this county road beside Rooster Tail. We all followed him. We had all these people pulling expensive boats and driving Corvettes and stuff. We kept going and going, then the guy who was in front pulled over on the side of the road. There was not much room, so he was on the grass on the side of the road. The older guy explained to everyone if we should turn around or something because we had been driving a while. Maybe we had missed a turn or something. We pulled passed a turn and there was a house up on a hill, but we were on the county road. While he was still talking to us, we saw a tractor come down and go to the field across from us. A couple guys suggested maybe the tractor driver was working his field on a Sunday and we could ask him a question. The man was riding up and down the field. Then someone noticed that he had a shotgun sitting on his lap and he was watching us. So, the older guy said,

The Inspiring Story of Lannie Dennis

"You all just be cool. I will get some directions." The guy on the tractor comes over to where we were, but not onto the road. Let me say this: the people who invited us down from Rooster Tail were white and good people. And the guy on the tractor and the people in the house were white. When the older guy was talking to the guy on the tractor, he told him that the guy from Rooster Tail had told them to come down and look for water where we could launch the boats and wait for him. We were still on the main road. We were on the right road. The older guy who was with us told the one on the tractor what we were there for, and asked if he knew if the boat launch was down this way. He replied that he didn't know and that we couldn't stay where we were. Our guy said this is a county road and the guy from Rooster Tail said he would be along with his boat about 15 minutes. The guy on the tractor said again that we couldn't stay there and then he raised his rifle up on his arm. The older guy with us said, "Everyone get in your car, don't say anything. Just turn around because we are heading back to Rooster Tail."

At this time, while we were down the road, a car pulled up in the driveway of the house on the hill. And before we got into our cars, there came three or four people up on the hill looking down at us. Now, we are trying to all turn around with boats behind our cars on a one lane county road. Of course, the car I was riding in was in the back, and I was in the backseat on the passenger side.

We started turning around. A couple of cars had to pull into the driveway to turn around. Some of them turned around in the middle of the road. The car I happened to be in (I think it was a 63 or 64 Chevy) had to back into the driveway to turn around. When he backed in and got ready to pull forward out of the turn, I heard something like shooting, and something hit the car. Everyone started to panic trying to get their boat out, because someone was shooting at us. The thing I don't understand is that the tractor guy who was close to us with his rifle did not shoot at us. I will come back to you later and tell you why I brought this up.

No one had any cell phones back during those days. Maybe some CBs. We haul-tailed it back to Rooster Tail to call the police. So, they took care of that, they told the guy at Rooster Tail and he said he couldn't believe it. When we looked at the car that we were in, let me say, my mother had to have been praying for me, because I was not that close to God then. There was a hole in the truck of the car, the bullet must have hit the vein in the back of the car and stopped there, because it was on my side and it would have come straight in my back. The 63 or 64 Chevy had the vein in the trunk. And no one of us

The Inspiring Story of Lannie Dennis

had any weapons.

If that wasn't crazy enough, when the police arrived, they wanted to lock up the driver of the car I was in, because the people at the house had called the police too and said that the guy in the car was harassing them. One policeman walked over to the car that had got shot at while another police officer was at the house. He said that it was a 30x30 rifle which is used to hunt deer with. They would have put a hole in me and the person in front of me, too!

Our driver said that he wanted to press charges on them. So, now the people at the house told the police that the car we seen earlier that went up to the house, was bringing their grandfather home from the hospital and he was the one that had shot at us. They stated that he was 99 years old and he had grabbed the rifle and had shot at us. So, if someone was harassing them or saying something, wouldn't the guy on the tractor have heard it, since he was right there closer to us? He didn't take any shots. Of course, the police arrested and locked up my driver! Luckily, these guys would always bring plenty of money in case their boats broke down or something. Whatever the bond was, they were able to put it up the same day.

MOTORCYCLE ORGANIZATION

I was in an organization called, "Super Natural Gas." It was a motorcycle organization in Shadyside. I did not have a motorcycle at that time, but I had a Trans Am. We used to rent places out and have dances with live bands. I can't remember all the bands, but it was all the latest bands from Annapolis and the surrounding area. One of the bands I met was Licyndiana, it was the Phillips brothers from out of Crownsville, Maryland. Lloyd Phillips was the manager at that time. They played good music, like Earth, Wind and Fire music. A lot of music that the other bands were playing wasn't that type of music. So, we formed a good connection. Because of him, I got to meet the other brothers and band members and grew to know them very well.

After a while, Orlando Phillips took over

managing them. He and I really hit it off. We started hanging out together. We became close friends like brothers. I got to know their parents, sister & cousins; we all became family. If I am not mistaking, one of our events was at the Black Stallion ranch. We used to have 2 or 3 bands at one time. We had Rock bands and Soul, R&B, Jazz, you name it, we had it. At our events we had all types of music. Then, Licyndiana got a record deal. Then, Lionel Job out of New York, became their manager and they changed their name to Starpoint.

If you meet any of them and ask them how they got the name Starpoint, it was ironic. The people that made up Starpoint were Renee Diggs, Ernesto Phillips, George Phillips, Orlando Phillips, Greg Phillips and Ky Adeyemo. Sometimes, they would hire extra musicians when they did live shows. I had the opportunity and was blessed to be able to travel with them at times. I took a lot of pictures and live videos while they practiced and some while they played live. I had the opportunity to meet other artists, Prince, Luther Vandross, Don Cornelius, Kool & the Gang, and a lot more. I was with them when they performed on Soul Train. They also appeared on Soap Opera shows and sang their hit song, Object of My Desire.

I would like to dedicate this section of my book to Starpoint, especially to Ernesto and Renee who went home to be with the Lord. I just had so much fun with them. George, Orlando and I would usually hang out a lot. Greg was the drummer, and man, could he play those drums! He is still performing today. Orlando played saxophone, bass guitar, keyboard, steel drums and he also sang. He is also still performing today. George and the rest are still writing songs and help other artists today. I thank God for all of them. I guess it comes from being around musicians in my early years, like Clarence Johnson (Snake), Leslie Gross, Glenn Thompson, Reginal Thompson & Phillip Pinkney. There were a couple bands that came out of Shadyside, Maryland like Pipe Dreamer, the Vandikes and other names I can't remember right now. I was blessed.

CANCER

In January of 2018, I started having problems with my stomach again. I was in the hospital for a week in January and a week in February. In March, my wife and I vacationed in Williamsburg, Virginia. While arriving on our vacation, my stomach began to be upset. Our plans were to go to Busch Gardens. It was a Sunday when we arrived in Virginia and we were supposed to be there for a week. Unfortunately, we came back home early because I was so sick. By that Wednesday morning, I thought I was feeling a little bit better, so we went to Busch Gardens. As soon as we went through the park gates, I got sick again; I was running to the bathroom, throwing up, having diarrhea and severe pain.

One of the park maintenance ladies approached

us after I came out of the bathroom, because I was looking so bad and bent over. She probably saw the concern on my wife's face. She asked if we needed any assistance. And we did. She called the medics and they responded within ten minutes. I thank God for using her to help me. The medic in the park called for transportation for me. They drove us to the First Aide station to make sure I was okay. The medic drove us to our car. You can't tell me that the Lord wasn't with us. You will never guess what the medic's last name was. It was, "Lord," and spelled the same way. He even got us complimentary tickets to return on another day, when I felt better.

After I got back home, I did feel better, but I returned to the hospital again and again with unbearable pain and vomiting and diarrhea. The doctors could not give me a diagnose of what was going on. They always fall back on my Crohn's Disease or Pancreatic until the blood works comes back and rules them out. By me having Crohn's, and they thought that was what it was, they did a colonoscopy. That's when they found that my Crohn's was still in remission. My Gastro doctor, Dr. G, was thinking about doing an endoscopy a couple months before, but didn't want to do it because part of my stomach was already gone and he didn't want to irritate the area or cause more damage. My Gastro doctor gave me the name of an Endoscopy doctor to make an appointment. I was supposed to see him the next week, but I got sick again. I went back in the hospital on a Saturday and had some tests and fluids. On that Monday, the doctor came in and did the Endoscopy. As soon as they finished the test, they gave me lunch, which was a salad. I got sick again about 15 minutes later, unbearable pain and vomiting and diarrhea. I was in so much pain that I just asked the Lord to take it away from me. I found out later that I shouldn't even have had any raw vegetables with all that was going on in my stomach.

I went home and waited for my results. When my Gastro doctor called, he said he needed to see me right away. I felt that he didn't have good news for me. Either way, I was trusting the Lord. My wife and I went to the appointment. It was during this appointment that my doctor informed me that I had stomach cancer. I simply said, "Okay, what does that mean or what do I have to do?" One good thing about this whole situation is that Dr. G has been my doctor since 1988. He was so sad and broken about the news. He is the type of doctor that cares about his patients. He gave me the name of an oncologist surgeon. He said it was good how well I was taking the news.

We immediately called our son, Cory, because

he wanted to know the results of the test. We told him about an oncology surgeon. I was out taping some Coffee Talk Episodes when my wife was trying to make an appointment with the oncology surgeon, but could not get an appointment for at least a month. By Cory working on the Govenor's campaign, he had met a lot of people. One of those people was Dr. Bhandari, who was also the Govenor's oncologist. He and Cory became friends. Dr. Bhandari set up for me to see a surgeon the very next day. After we met with the surgeon, I had my port inserted in a couple days so that I could start my chemo treatments right away.

    I had chemo treatments every other week on Wednesdays. I needed to receive chemo for another 24 hours, so they hooked up a pump that I took home and ran all night. Then, on that Thursday, I had to return the pump and get any fluids to help with dehydration. Either way, I had to take the pump back. On Fridays, I had to return again for a Neulasta shot that helped with my red/white blood cells. This was a 3-day process. Thank God for my wife's boss letting her work from home during this time. That was a tremendous blessing. I don't know what I would have done if she couldn't have been with me. Plus, dealing with Dr. Bhandari's staff, they were so wonderful to me (and all the patients that they had, too). Remember, I was in a lot of pain and discomfort, and on a lot of medicine. They treated everyone with kindness and professionalism.

After the chemo treatments, I felt tired that entie week. My hair started to fall out two weeks after my first chemo treatment. I knew my hair was going to do that. I thought I was ready for it. When I took my hand and rubbed across my head, my hair came out in my hand. Tears started coming down my face. I had to get myself together. My wife shaved my head. I got sick a couple of times, throwing up. I couldn't drink anything cool or touch anything cool; this was from the effects of the strong chemo I was receiving. Before those effects could wear off, it was time to do another round of chemo. That was hard, because I like everything that I drink to be cold, such things like Italian ice, smoothies from Smoothie King, Slurpees, etc., all that cold stuff. When I touched something cold or put something cold in my hand, it felt like hot ice. It is hard to explain, but I was told that part of the chemo I was getting made this happen. I was told that if I were to drink something cold, it could burn my throat. I did try the ice in my hand, and it was definitely burning, so I was not even going to try to drink anything cold. So, I had to drink only room temperature drinks. Even water I had at room temperature; I couldn't drink much. I needed the fluids to keep my strength. The chemo treatments made my food taste different. So, I had no urge to eat and still don't eat much. I received four rounds of chemo to try and shrink the Stomach Cancer, so that they might not have to remove all of my stomach. I had to wait a month from my last chemo to have my surgery. During that time, my hair started to grow back; only this time, it was straight instead of the curly locks I used to have.

I had surgery on Nov 19, 2018. A couple days before my surgery, Bari called and said he had a surprise for me. He was coming to my house to pick me up. We drove to a private air strip. We walked through the building. The next thing I knew he said, they were flying me to New York to get something to eat. We were going on a private jet. It was an 8-passenger Citation X, complements of Daniel Nainan. He and Bari are friends; Daniel is a comedian. Daniel has been following my cancer journey through "Coffee Talk" and talking to Bari. Daniel wanted to do this for us, before I had surgery. That was another blessing. I laughed after Bari said that was one thing he could mark off of his bucket list. Then he asked, "How about you?" I started laughing, because it wasn't ever on my bucket list. That was something I never thought I would do. Like I said, you never know what the Lord has planned for you. I felt like a king on that jet.

Lannie on private plane

The surgery was supposed to take three hours, but it took five hours. It went well, but they ended up removing the rest of the stomach, pancreas and spleen which they had not planned on doing. However, the cancer was in these areas too, so they removed them. I stayed in the hospital for five days. And once again, I could not have done this without God, my wife and family being there by my side for support. I know it was hard on my wife and family, but I had so many people praying for me, such as our three sons and family members, my church family at Severn Run Church and Cory's co-workers at the State House. I know the Governor and First Lady were praying for me because they called me. They were really supportive. The Governor had gone through a bout of cancer, too. That was a big lift for me, how God used so many people to talk to me thru them. I was blessed again; people were at the hospital at 5:30 in the morning with me. My wife, Sharon, my Pastor and friend, Drew Shofner, my sister in Christ, Gwen Hubbard, my brother and sister in Christ, Larry and Hedy Nelson, our son, Cory Dennis and my sister-in-law, Sharlene Savage.

There were some rough nights in the hospital. I had excruciating pain and reactions from the pain medicine. Thank God once again, for my wife was able to stay at the hospital with me. I am so glad she was, because the medicine had me hallucinating at times. By her being there, I could call on her or just see her laying on the couch helped me to stay focused and get my focus back on the Lord. It's great to have someone with you while you are going through this degree of pain and uncertainty.

I was on a feeding tube and I was very weak, but they got me up the next day after surgery. They wanted to get me to start walking right away. I first started off with a walker. By the second day, I was walking with a cane. Plus, because of my blindness, my wife had to get familiar with my feeding tube procedure, medicine and daily bandage changing. She did a great job. I know it couldn't be easy. I thank the Lord for being with her. She was so calm; if she wasn't, you would have never known it. That is why I give all glory to the Lord. This journey was rough, dealing with blindness and out of my comfort zone, being taking to other rooms for test and not being able to see where I was, and on pain medicine that did not help. But I knew the Lord was with us.

I was finally released to go home after being in the hospital for five days. The doctors said that was really good, because I was progressing so well. I had home care which was a nurse coming in to check my vital signs and to check if I needed anything in regards to my feeding tube. I also had a physical therapist, because I wasn't walking that well in the hospital. I was off balance. The physical therapist came in one day and I answered the door. He said he came to see Lannie. I told him I was Lannie. He was amazed from the report he got from the hospital. I was only home for two or three days when he came for the first time and saw me walking, and he said I didn't need any assistance, except for my blind cane. Thank the Lord that my walking had improved that well. God is so good. The nurse came twice a week for three weeks. She said I was recovering so well that she didn't need to keep coming. That is why I thank the Lord for always being with me. I still had pain and was still using the feeding tube. I had to regulate what I could eat and not eat while still having the feeding tube, trying to see what my stomach could hold. I was told I would probably have the feeding tube until after I finished my chemo treatments.

The feeding tube wasn't that bad, but wasn't that great either, it played with my mind. It was something I had to get used to. Sometimes, we had to laugh and cry a lot.

I had people wanting to come visit me at home, like Joe & Anna Hall, Larry & Hedy Nelson. Pastor Drew and Gwen Hubbard brought us crab cakes and food. A group of my CMA (Christian Motorcyclist Association) Bayside Believers Chapter members came a couple times to the house to pray for me. It was good to have them there. They were a blessing to us and still are.

Lannie with CMA Members

My wife told me afterwards that it wasn't easy learning how to maintain the feeding tube, getting all the supplies for it and managing my medications; like what to take if I felt a certain way or the other. She did it all without any complaints. She always tells people that, "I would do the same for her."

Four weeks after my surgery, I started my next round of chemo. My hair started to fall out again. I had to have my head shaved again. Only this time it didn't grow back as quick. Like before, I had to bring the pump home for 24 hours of chemo. Also, I had to connect the feeding tube every night. That ran for eight hours. The first night was bringing the pump home and then connecting the feeding tube. It was a chore getting to and from the bathroom. The feeding tube was on a pole with rollers and the chemo pump was in a carrier bag around my neck. The first night of the chemo, I had to drag all this stuff to the bathroom several times a night.

One episode I had coming out of the bathroom, trying my best to be as quiet as possible, not to wake up Sharon, but my foot got tangled up in the feeding tube and the tube pulled right out of my stomach. I had to wake up Sharon to turn the feeding tube machine off and patch up the hole in my stomach. We had to call the emergency number that we were given. They wanted to know if it was leaking a lot, but it was not. So, they instructed us just to put a bandage on it. We had to go back to the hospital to have it looked at to see if they had to put it back in. The feeding tube was mostly for nutrition. Thank God that I was eating enough and was recovering enough that they did not have to put it back in. Where the feeding tube came out, it leaked constantly every time I ate, bent over, or drank anything, for about a month and a half, until it finally healed. It was hard for it to heal while doing the chemo. It was hard to socialize during that time too, because the hole would start leaking and getting my clothes soiled. I had two holes in me, my port for the chemo and the feeding tube.

Let me say this, battling with cancer was not a walk in the park. You have stuff happening to your body all the time and foreign objects in your body that you are not used to. Most of the time the medication made you not feel like yourself. A lot of times I didn't want people to see me, not because of how I looked, but because I would get sick while they were visiting me. Sometimes when people would say they are coming over, I had to tell them to come by another day, because I wasn't feeling well. But that is okay, because if you are sick, you are sick; just let them know. You don't need any more stress on you. You are dealing with the illness and you have to focus on getting your strength back to good health. If you have to do it alone, that is what you have to do. You can do it. Keep fighting, don't give up. If you have family or someone with you, it will help you get through the hard, painful times. I made my mind up that I wasn't going to give up, no matter what. I did what I could do, and what I couldn't do, I let God handle it. During my second chemo treatment, I started getting sick all the time. It wasn't like the first treatment. The neuropathy had started right after the first round of chemo, but by then it had worsened.

Chemo changed the skin color of my hands. I lost my hair and had reactions to medications. The mental and physical anguish on my body was enormous. I could not do that without God and my supporters. I was trying to stay away from the pain medicine, Oxycodone, because I didn't want to get addicted to it. I've heard of people getting addicted to it, however, I needed to take it for the pain. I didn't want to have bad effects from it. Even now I can take it for my neuropathy.

I would have my chemo treatment on Wednesdays. And by Friday I would be feeling sick until at least Monday or Tuesday. Sometimes, I had to go back to the Oncologist office to get fluid because I was dehydrated from vomiting. No matter what, my wife always had my back. When I started feeling better it was time for another treatment. I had them every two weeks. I couldn't get to the last treatment fast enough.

Finally, I had my last treatment of chemo on Feb. 21, 2019. It was time to ring the bell. The day I rang the bell, I was glad my mother and sister could be there. My Pastor and a sister from church was there, too, along with our son, Cory, and my wife, Sharon.

Ringing the Bell with Dr. Bandhari & Staff

I was blessed to have my friend and co-worker from "Coffee Talk" there to video the day. If you want to see the video, go to YouTube: Ringing the bell, New beginnings.

After ringing the bell, I realized more vividly that

I got through this journey with Christ's help and His mercy. Sometimes, you don't realize how God is on your side until you are fully through a situation. Just two weeks after ringing the bell, I had to have another PETSCAN to see if they had gotten all of the cancer cells. Praise God, I am cancer free, the victory belongs to Him!

I remember calling my mother and asking her to pray for me, knowing that she has been praying all the time. I called my sister knowing the same thing. If I remember correctly, either from pain or sickness or running to the bathroom, I just know I was getting depressed and tired. That's okay, as long as I didn't stay that way. Thank God that Sharon was always there picking up the pieces and telling me she's got my back. My Church family always was there, too. I also remember I used to call Joe Hall all the time; he would be at work asking everyone there to pray for me, especially at times when I just didn't know what to do or how to handle the pain. As I was experiencing the pain, I know they couldn't do anything about it, but it was just great to have them listen to me and pray for me. Jackie, Barbara Lee and Betty extended prayers for me as well; they were there for me and lent a listening ear. Thank God for all of my prayer warriors.

My burden through this "blessing" is that I now have nerve damage in my feet and hands:

neuropathy. The only way I get through all this is by staying focused on the blessings not the burden. I've learned that with blessings come burdens. I was told that the neuropathy could last 18 months or more. If it lasts any longer than that, then it would mean it may last forever. My feet and hands constantly hurt and are swollen all day, every day. One day, I didn't realize I had my shoes on the wrong feet. I have to say this: sometimes God stops us from getting into the fire, and sometimes He lets us go through the fire, so we can have a testimony for His Glory. Even through the fire He is with you. Also, I would like to say that what happened to me during my chemo treatment may not happen with others. A friend of mine told me that his mother and sister, couldn't wait to do chemo. They never had any problems and never got sick. Everyone has their own individual experience with chemo. I can only say, with the chemo, my cancer is gone.

    I had another great opportunity on May 22, 2019, to go down to the Naval Academy in Annapolis to watch the Blue Angels again with my wife, Sharon, and our friend, Bari. We did the same thing the previous year. Our friend, Diane, who is blind, was able to go with us on this occasion. Bari was taking her hand and using her hand jesters like the Blue Angels when they were flying around, up and down and sideways. They did this because a lot of us suffer with vision impairment, but there are a lot of things that can be done to help us see. I, myself, can see a little bit, but I had the updated Iris Vision to look through. With the updated version I could take a picture and save it, then save it to my computer. The picture quality was great, just like you are taking a picture from your camera. We had a great time watching the Blue Angels that day. It was a beautiful day and the weather was great. There were a lot of people there. Diane enjoyed the tour we gave her. As usual, Bari did a Facebook live video at the end of the day. It was a long day, but it was great. We ate in Dahlgren Hall on the base. This was 2019 graduation week, so there were a lot of people on the base. Most people had to walk on the base, but we were able to drive onto the base, because we are sponsors and Naval Club members. Next year we are planning on getting a 15-passenger van and bring some of the other blind and low vision people to see the Blue Angels. This would be no charge to them, complements of the Low Vision Specialist of Maryland and Virginia. That is their goal, to be there and serve the community.

Blue Angels flying over Naval Academy Stadium

Me, Dr. Bari and Naval Academy Cadets

I don't take life for granted and you shouldn't either. Last year, when I was there, I didn't even know that I had cancer. I didn't find out until the end of July of that same year that I had cancer. Life is too short and that's why I pray this testimony will be of help to someone. I look at this book as more than just a book, but a testimony of encouragement. So, it really isn't about me, but it's about the Lord and the people He used around me. When you read my son, Cory's poem at the end of this book, you will see why I made that statement.

My hand is still bothering me, at the tip of my fingers where I am experiencing numbness and tingling. My feet also still bother me; feels like I am walking on eggshells at times. Today is June

19, 2019, and it is 90 degrees outside and my feet feel like they are stuck in the snow for 3 or 4 hours freezing like they are frostbitten.

I remember one day while we were in Florida, I had my shoes on the wrong feet for half of a day, before my wife looked down and saw them. My fingernails on my hands were falling off, too, but I now see where they are growing back (praise God). My oncologist and neurologist both say it is from the chemo (keep in mind, they gave me a high dose of chemo). I had eight treatments; four treatments before the surgery and the other four treatments after the surgery. They took all of my stomach out, then made me a stomach out of my intestine. They told me it's only been about three months since the last chemo and I need to give it 18 months; if it is still there after 18 months, I'll probably have to live with it for the rest of my life.

Please remember that just because this happened to me doesn't mean it's going to happen to someone else. So, even though I had a high dose of chemo, and all of what I'm sharing may be scary to many of you, just bear in mind that I am gradually getting back to my old self. I am so grateful that the Lord gave me a second chance to live – thank God! Now, it's up to me what I do with this second chance. I would love to help others and to let them know it may not be easy at times, but with the Lord, family and friends, you can do it. Notice, I didn't say that you will not get frustrated, depressed or even feel like giving up at times. The main thing for us is to try and stay focused on living. As long as I'm alive, I believe God has need of me to be an encouragement to others. It may even be that they can see the Lord's strength working through me during my most difficult and painful moments. He undoubtedly used my wife and seemed to give her supernatural strength and love to assist me. Without her help I know the intensity of the pain would have been ten times more severe. Without God using her, I don't know what I would have done. I thank the Lord for her dearly and repeat this multiple times throughout this book, because I realize the extent of her dedication to me. Her love toward me is a marquee example of God's love for the world.

My mom, my sister, my kids, my pastor and my Church family and so many people were praying for me during my fight with cancer. If you're battling cancer or having a difficult time in life with any issue, I pray the Lord will give you people who will support you. You're going to need to talk to someone and tell them the truth about how you feel. This is therapeutic and will strengthen you, especially during those moments where you feel emotionally pressured into giving up. Definitely tell the Lord how you feel. He already knows, but He want you to talk to Him just like you are talking to your best friend, a brother or a dad. Ponder on this, if the Lord is your friend, then think about the friends that you have now and how often do you talk to them? I am pretty sure it is not once a month or once a year. So, the Lord wants to hear from us, if we trust Him.

Something came to mind just now about my sister, Shirley Ann, as I am writing this book. She was there during the time I have been battling this cancer. I think I was in stage 4; the outcome didn't look good for me. I was thinking about my sister, because we had just lost our older brother about four years ago from a heart attack. I started thinking about how she was concerned about losing her little brother. Well, she held up pretty well (at least around me she did). Her strength really helped me through this journey. If you're reading this book, I say from the depths of my heart, "Thank you sis, I love you."

Left to right: *Cory, Lannie, Dr. Bhari, Mom and Sharon at Ringing the Bell Ceremony*

Me, Sharon and Cory at Chemo Treatment

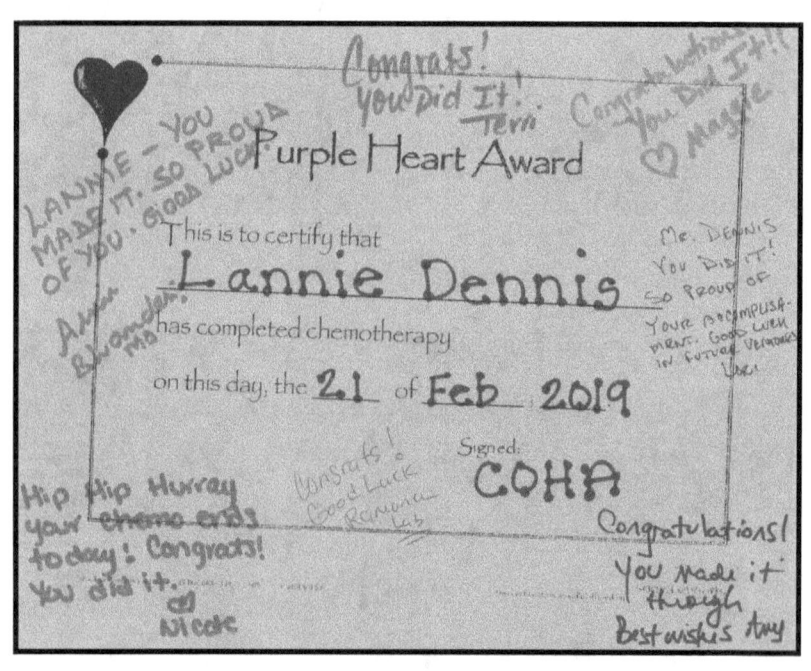

Certificate from when I completed Chemotherapy

BLINDNESS

I always had problems with my eyes since the 80s. They watered all the time. I had to change a few doctors because of my insurance companies. Finally, my primary eye doctor had sent me to a couple of specialists. At first, they couldn't find anything wrong when I did a field test. I remember sitting there and hearing the examiner lady say, "Click the button when you see the light flash." She then said, "It is ready now, you can click the button." I said, "Okay." After a few minutes she instructed me again that I could click the button when I see the light flashing. A couple of seconds after that I finally clicked the button, because I could see the lights. However long the test was, I finished. This was like on a Monday.

This test was performed for my Optometrist.

The technician asked me when I should see my Optometrist again. I told her that I had an appointment to see my Optometrist the next Friday. I was told then that she would get my test results later during the day and I would get a call the next day. The technician said that if the doctor didn't call me by tomorrow, then I should call her. That's when I realized, that earlier when I hadn't clicked the button, I must have missed a lot of the light flashing. In other words, she wanted me to get back to my optometrist ASAP, so that the results could get to my Ophthalmologist. His name was Dr. Price. I was his patient for about six years or more. He always kept telling me, "Lannie, something is not right." He could never get my vision to the right focus. He had tried and had sent me to specialists for many years. He really was a good doctor, because he kept trying.

Dr. Price sent me to another Specialist, Dr Kelman. He repeated the field test and performed a special cornea test. He also suggested I see Dr. Sunness at the Hoover Low Vision Center at GBMC. There, she gave me multiple test (and I do mean MULTIPLE test), but could not give me a diagnosis. Some people say it was macular degeneration or something similar. However, Dr. Sunness said that it was not that. It was close to these, but not it. Dr. Sunness prescribed some glasses that had just come out which made me close one eye to focus on anything. They hooked on to my current glasses. It did help a little. It was like looking out of a hole. We tried that for about a year or more. It was cumbersome. I was telling my wife that it would work better if it had a lens on both eyes.

We flew into Orlando Airport on our Anniversary. I was doing something, and my wife walked up to me with a gentleman by her side. She said that he was interested in my eyeglasses that I had on. He was a low vision specialist doctor. He was telling me that they used to sell that type of eyeglasses. But now they had a new magnifier one that fit into the eyeglasses instead of over top the glasses and it was for both eyes. I was definitely interested in that. He asked me where I lived and I informed him that I resided in Maryland. He was located in Las Vegas. To show you how God works, he was leaving to go back home and we had just landed. He said that they had just come from a conference that they hold every year. They review the new low vision devices that are out. This conference is for doctors that specialize in low vision. He gave me the name of the Low Vision Specialist doctor in Maryland. His name is Dr. Thomas Azman. He had an office in Timonium, Maryland. Look at God!

Like I said we had just landed in Florida. So, as soon as we got to our resort, I called and made an appointment with Dr. Thomas Azman at Low Vision Specialist of Maryland and Virginia. They scheduled my appointment for November 22, 2013. This is the day that Dr. Tom introduced me to the telescope glasses. I remember when I first tried them on. I started crying, because I could see more, and images were much sharper.

These are specially prescribed eyeglasses and I literally had them on! At that time, I was driving; I had a motorcycle (trike).

Me and Sharon riding on my Trike

They increased my vision so much that I could read street signs and was very comfortable driving.

Before I got my telescope glasses, I noticed my eyesight was getting worse. How they would work is that the magnifier is made into the glasses. The glasses have to be made specifically for your visual needs. You have to be tested to see what power strength you need. On top of that, I have dry eyes, meaning that my eyes watered a lot. As great as these glasses were, neither my insurance nor Medicare would pay anything for them. These special made eyeglasses cost anywhere from $3,000 upward to $6,000 dollars. If you just wanted them for reading, then you could get a different prescription. Usually, if you go to a low vision specialist and you have some vision, they can help you with a device. Dr. Tom asked me if he could give people my name that were interested in the eyeglasses. Of course, I said, "Yes," to testify about them. I wanted to give back to my community, because I have been so blessed. I always tell people that this is how it worked for me, even though it may not be the same for you.

Dr. Tom always said he wanted me to meet his son, Bari, who was the marketing person for Low Vision Specialist. With my upbeat personality, he thought that we would be a good match working together. Bari was visiting senior centers and talking to people about new devices that were coming out to help people with low vision, which I thought was a great thing. They asked me if I wanted to do a TV commercial about the binocular glasses. That is when I met Bari, who was in charge of all of that. Glenda and I did the TV commercial in February 2018. Glenda is a low vision patient also that uses the binocular glasses. Bari and I have been partners ever since. The reason I jumped on board is because it wasn't just selling devices, but it was getting the news out that would help many people.

I had the telescope eyeglasses for about four years, when I felt that my vision declining again. We did another eye test about a month later. That is when I was told I was legally blind. I could see some things up close. I had to stop driving, and that was a whole other thing for me, especially my motorcycle and hanging out with my Christian Motorcyclist Association (CMA) chapter members. Sharon and I were members and still are members of the Bayside Believers chapter. I really had to go to God about this. He really helped me to get through this. When I rode my bike, I felt so close to God, free and at peace with Him. I had to sell my motorcycle. I did that in a couple of weeks after finding out about my blindness. It was just too hard having it in the parking lot and not being able to ride it safely. Like I said, I can see some. It was hard to comprehend, because it was such a lifestyle change for me. We went on many adventures with our Bike association, like trips to Maine, Shenandoah State

Park and Cape May.

Sometimes I didn't even want to go outside, even to go to the store with Sharon. I started to get depressed. I had to talk to the Lord to give me strength and to fight the depression, and to get myself moving again. Like I said before, I am an outgoing person and love to talk to people. If someone is sad, I try to lift them up. When I went to funerals, outside gatherings or anyplace there was a lot of people, I couldn't tell who was there, unless they came up to me or my wife would tell me who they were. Sometimes, I would find out after I got home that someone was there that I would like to have talked to.

Being blind, I miss the view of places I go to, because I can't see where I am. I can see figures, but can't make them out. A lot of things are just a blur. The telescope eyeglasses could only help me see just a little bit further at this point. Especially with the TV, it was so frustrating not being able to make things out. I had to realize this is something I have to deal with and be thankful to God for what I do have. At least I can see a little bit. I think about other people who are blind and can't see anything, like my friend Diane and some people I meet at conferences. Some cannot see their grandkids, like when they play sports and things on those lines. I have been so blessed with my wife, family and friends. I thank God for them being there with me.

At this time there were some other eyeglasses out called, "E-Sight." They cost from $12,000 to $15,000. Like I said before, my insurances would not pay for any of this. During one of my eye examinations with Dr. Tom, he began telling me about a new device that was coming out called, "Iris Vision" and he wanted me to try them. They had a demo device there and Steven Azman was telling me about it. Their office was trying to get me a device, but Iris Vision was so new; there weren't too many of them out in the marketplace. I was waiting for them to come in, but after about 4-5 months, I went on the manufacturer's website. I let them know I was trying to get one from Low Vision Specialist of Maryland & Virginia and that I had been waiting for one. The manufacturers said they were trying to get them out to the office, but they couldn't manufacture them fast enough. He did agree, however, to get mine moving through Low Vision Specialist of Maryland & Virginia. I finally received mine! With the telescope glasses and the Iris Vision, it was like a new beginning again.

Bari and I had hit it off so well that Bari asked if I wanted to go to a conference at the School of the Blind in Baltimore. I was more than happy to do that. There were a lot of vendors set up there for the event. The table beside us was Sprint; they had some device to help the blind to use on their phones. That is where I met Diane. She is blind and she gets around just great. Bari has known her for a while. It seemed like she and I and Bari just clicked. We do a lot of laughing and joking, and I feel good around them. This particular day it began to snow, so we left the conference early. Bari was giving Diane a ride home that day. He asked us if we wanted to stop at Starbucks. I remember the funny part is that Bari let us out front of the door while he parked the car, he told us to go on in. Now try to imagine this, both of us trying to get inside the Starbucks - you talk about blind leading the blind! How were we going to get inside the place? I can't see that well and she can't see at all. We laughed so hard 'til my stomach started to hurt.

When Bari came into the store, he got our drinks for us. Diane asked me where I was raised. I started telling her how I was raised on a dairy farm in Shadyside, Maryland, with my mother and father, Carrie and Lannie (Thomas) Dennis, my older brother Jimmy and older sister Ann (Shirley), my grandfather and aunt. The owner of the farm was Benny Crowner. Later on, the Weems took over the farm – Ray, Richard and Dale Weems. I told her how I had a great time with my friend, Mousie (his given name was actually Rupport Nick). Anyway, my cousins would come over, Willie, Walter and

Sydnie. Sometimes my aunt Olivia and her husband Wilson Scott. I remember going down to the barn where Jimmy and my father were milking the cows. Then, I began to milk the cows. I loved driving the tractor around the field. Once when I was milking a cow, it kicked me in the mouth. My mouth was swollen for a long time. Back in those days we weren't cousins, we were like one big family. Also, back then, I can remember my father doing a lot of bartering.

Me at Starbucks in New York

While I was telling her this, Bari was recording us on his telephone. We had a good time talking. We took Diane home while we went back to the office. Bari was trying to show me the recording on the computer. I had my Iris Vision on. Bari said something like, "This should be on YouTube." He asked, "What can we call it?" Next, he said, "Let's call it 'Coffee Talk with Lannie D.' That became a regular Vlog. At the time I am writing this, we have about 20 episodes and 2,000 followers, all who we've gained in one year.

We use Coffee Talk with Lannie D as a service to the community to get the word out about new technology for people with low vision. We also went to the Library for the Blind and Disabled sharing with people about free help and resources, such as books on tape and braille. They teach people to read braille there. I was shown how people narrate the books on tape. In fact, this is one of the episodes we have on Coffee Talk with Lannie D. Now you can see why I jumped on board with Low Vision Specialist and Bari. Bari has a heart for the people and wants to get the word out. They have a low vision shop where people can come and try out the devices. Also, what I like about Bari is that he doesn't push people into buying things if it's not going to help you. If his shop doesn't sell a particular device, he would tell you where you can get it.

Thank God, there is a lot of technology coming out to help the blind and low vision people today like the Iris Vision that I have; it really helped me a lot. I think I was the first one on the East Coast to get one. Like I said, it may not work for some people, but over 2000 people have them now, and they have only been on the market for about 4 years (I think). I started crying when I put them on. When people ask me about them, I say, "If you are not blind, and you go into a dark room where you can't see your hand in front of your face, and someone turns the light on for you; that is how they work for me. They are like a big screen TV in comparison to an iPhone screen.

I take my Iris Vision everywhere. I went to one of my grandson's football games. He was about 9 years old at that time. I had been to one before, but could never see him. I could only hear what other people were saying about him making tackles and touchdowns. I went to the game with my Iris Vision one time. I was standing against the fence where he was playing. I could actually see him out there in the field. That day, I watched him intercept the ball and run down the field with the ball. It was so amazing to see. Family members were there, and someone walked up to me while I still had the eyeglasses on and said, "I know you are crying." And they were right. To be able to see that moment with my grandson was without words. Just recently, I went to my great nephew, Carson's, T-Ball game. I wore my Iris Vision eyeglasses. I would have never seen him play without my eyeglasses on.

The Inspiring Story of Lannie Dennis

Another thing I'd like to mention is that Sharon and I have been sponsoring midshipmen at the Naval Academy in Annapolis Maryland for about 10 years or more. Our youngest son graduated from the Naval Academy in 2015. The Blue Angels usually come a few days before graduation to do a demonstration. I went there a few years to watch them, but I couldn't see them very well. In 2018, we asked Bari if he wanted to go, because he had never been there before. He was very excited about that. We went down there and this was the first time I had my Iris Vision to watch the Blue Angels. In all those years of missing them before, this was the first time I could really see the Blue Angels and could see them clearly. I can't explain, but it felt so great that I could see them perform. That is why I thank God for all the new technology coming out to help the blind and low vision. Of course, Bari was doing some videoing while we toured him around before the demonstration started. That video is on another Coffee Talk vlog – "Blue Angels with Low Vision Specialist" on YouTube. Now, a year later, and we are more than excited to go watch them again with my Iris Vision

I would like to talk a little about the blind cane that blind people carry around with them. The one I have can be folded so I can carry in my bag or back pocket. Like I said, I am legally blind, but I can see some. That is what gets me frustrated a lot of times. Don't take this wrong, I thank God for being able to see some. I feel that many people may not understand and may need to be more educated on people who are blind but can see some. Sometimes, I don't need my blind cane. It was hard even for me to start to carry the cane until I looked at "Sam, the Blind Life" on why we should carry the cane. He is on YouTube also.

Lannie with blind stick boarding jet

First, let me say why some of it is frustrating. If it is bright outside, I may be able to see where I am going without the blind cane, unless I am walking down the sidewalk or someplace, I am not familiar with. Some people think that you are pretending like you are blind, but you are not. That is the hard part and it hurts. I heard about someone that could see a little like me, going into the store during the day. They had their blind cane folded up out of sight. When they went into the store, they opened their blind cane, because it was darker in the store than it was outside. They did their shopping, and when they came out of the store, they folded their cane up (like I do sometimes). Because it was lighter outside and they folded up their cane, someone walked up to them and said to them that they were pretending being blind. To us, that is insulting. This is just one example of some of the things that we go through. Probably, there are more people that think that same way but don't say anything; they just give you that look. I wouldn't know because I can't see their faces.

I remember what happened to me one day in the store. My wife and I were together. I had my blind cane folded where I placed in the shopping cart. I was pushing the cart, while my wife was in front of me leading the cart. We stopped at the jewelry case looking for a birthstone ring for me. While my wife was looking at the rings, someone was close enough to us where I could see their shadow, but couldn't make them out. So, I tried to move the cart some, because I didn't know if it was in their way or not. I heard this voice say, "No, you don't have to move it." They said it twice. I thought I recognized the voice, but wasn't for sure. It was my cousin, Harvey. He grabbed me from behind and gave me a bear hug. I hadn't seen him for quite a while. He was talking to my wife asking how we were doing. She told him that I was legally blind. He was shocked because he didn't know. Then, he said he owed me an apology. I asked why, because we always joked with each other (we used to work together). He said he was on the other side of the jewelry counter in the aisle way waving is hands and making faces at me. He thought I was ignoring him because I never responded to him. Then, he said to himself, "I am just going to pay for my stuff and get out of here." But then he thought, "Hell no, I am not letting him get away with this." That's when he came over to us, but he really came over to air me out. And that is why he was apologizing. This is what frustrates me – everyone doesn't know that I am blind. I wonder how many people have thought the same thing but didn't come over to see why I didn't speak. This is some of the things that we, who can see some, go through. I can only see someone if they are 3-4 feet in front of me. Even then, at times, I still cannot make out their faces. My sister-in-law actually did the same thing and she knows I am blind, and she was farther away from me than my cousin was.

    I make myself go out to places, because I refuse

to stay in the house. It is frustrating because it is not fun anymore. I have to stop even with my Iris Vision and look at things one at a time, that takes time. Or I have to ask my wife what each thing is that I am trying to look at. But it does save me money, if I can't see it, I can't buy it. I can understand because sometimes my wife forgets or doesn't know what I can and cannot see. Sometimes, she pulls me through the store 90 miles an hour. I wish it was a joke, but it's not. Sometimes, she points out an item saying it is over here or there or says, "Right there," which means nothing to me. But I love her dearly, she has been right there with me through all of this, Crohn's, blindness and cancer. Bari is a big help with my blindness, getting me out doing Coffee Talk, conferences and being around other people dealing with blindness too. We always support and raise awareness. We have a lot of speaking engagements letting people know what's out there to help them. That is why I am proud of being an ambassador for Low Vision Specialist of Maryland & Virginia.

I get frustrated at times being blind, but it can be used to help others. I just need to remember that it's not about me. We can be used by some of the trials we go through to help others. Some of the frustration comes from not being able to drive anymore. I was used to coming and going as I pleased; I would visit people when I wanted to visit them, etc. Now, I have to depend on my wife and others. My wife has never had any issues with taking me anywhere I wanted to go, but it is not the same as getting up and going by yourself. I know at times she probably doesn't feel like going when I want to go, but she does anyhow. She may not even want to go to places I want to go, but she never said anything. That is a lifestyle change, my friend, that you will have to get used to.

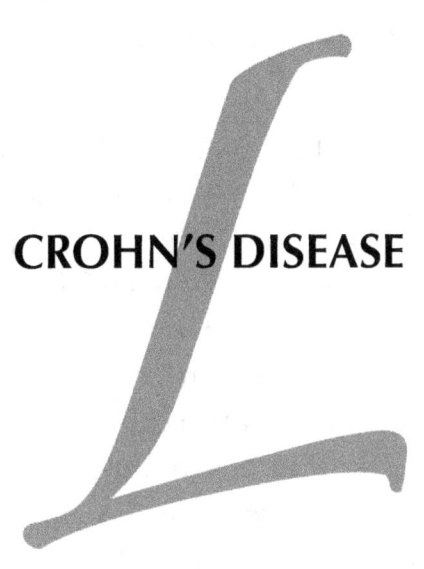

CROHN'S DISEASE

I was diagnosed with Crohn's disease in 1989 by Dr. G. I remember coming home from the doctors. Sharon and I were riding in the car, neither of us said anything. I had been having stomach problems since 1985. They took part of my stomach out in 1975, because they thought I had ulcers. I was in and out of the hospital for years not knowing what the problem was until I met Dr. G. (he is my gastroenterologist). He thought it was ulcerative colitis or Crohn's Disease. These two diseases are so close that it is hard to tell them apart. In 1989, Dr. G determined it was Crohn's Disease. At that time, they said I was in a high risk of getting colon cancer. I had just got married to my wife Sharon in November 1989. We wanted to have a child, but after we left the office, as I stated, neither one of us said anything. I told her that we would leave it in God's hands. We were going to have a child. Both of us already had sons, Troy and Louis, from two different relationships, but we wanted one together.

I started keeping record on how many times a day I was going to the bathroom. Sometimes, I would go 20-30 times a day. I know that is kind of hard to believe, but ask anyone who has Crohn's, when it flares up, bathroom visits happen more frequently than normal. Some people have asked me what Crohn's Disease feels like. I would tell them that, to me, it's like having the flu and you'd have to run to the bathroom, and also have a constant feeling of tiredness. When the Crohn's flared up, I would feel like that every day. Because of the severity of the illness, I was put on disability in 1989. When I would go to work, I'd get sick, go to the hospital and stay there for about two weeks getting IV's and fluids. During this time, they didn't know very much about Crohn's. I would work for about a month and then get sick again and start the same routine all over again. Thank God I had Long Term Disability Insurance. Like I said I was put on disability. Without that insurance, I don't know what would have happened. I had to apply for Social Security Disability in 1990, that was not approved until 1995. Once again, God looked out for me. I would have had to go 5 years without any income. I could have ended up homeless. Like my dad always would say, "We were too poor to have insurance, but to poor not to have insurance." He always reminded us that when you get a job make sure you get insurance. I think most of my family has this coverage now.

During this time with Crohn's Disease, I was still able to attend all of Troy's football and basketball games and Louis' baseball games. You still need to know where the bathrooms are at all the time.

In 1992, God blessed us with another son, Cory. I know I had to be focused, because I had the same routine of running to the bathroom and don't know when it was coming down on me. I always took extra clothes with me. Anywhere I went, I had to know where the bathrooms were. When, the Crohn's is not flared up, it's not too bad, but you still have to go to the bathroom, just not that many times. Your bowels can come down on you anytime, and unexpectedly. This has happened to me, but thank God it never happened while I was out of the house. It almost happened to me one time when I was going to see my Aunt and also pick up my cousin in Baltimore. I was on the express way. When I got to the exit, I just knew I wasn't going to make it. Once again, the Lord brought me through. When I came off the exit there was a McDonald's nearby. I made it to the bathroom there and was praying that all the stalls weren't being occupied. Thank God they weren't; I just made it.

As Cory got older, I had to stay focused on him more and not my illness. I thank God for him, because he helped me to focus on other things. I was getting depressed being home. It looked like nothing was wrong with me from the outside. Some people look at me like I was ducking work. The only thing about that is if I had a job, I couldn't do it. Not even a part time job flagging traffic or something. I could not be dependable because of my physical condition. I could be there today, but couldn't be there tomorrow. Or, I'd be there for two weeks, and then miss the next two weeks. When you work for someone, they need to know that you will be there. They can sympathize about your illness, but they cannot afford to lose money by keeping you on the job because they feel sorry for you.

The blessing was that I got to stay home and raise one of my sons. I joke with people and say that if he turned out bad, then I couldn't blame it on my wife, but he was with me from the day he was born. Staying home and raising Cory was a good thing for me. How many fathers would like to stay home with their child but have to go to work instead?

I remember someone asked me, "What do you do during the day?" I said, "I read my scripture and take care of my son." They said, "Oh, you are a babysitter." I said, "No, I am a father." I define a babysitter as a person who watches someone else's kid(s), not when you watch your own kid.

I was told about the 'terrible twos.' I was blessed by never having any problems with Cory, even when he turned two years old. The bad part was not taking him to the doctors, but holding him while the doctor gave him his needle. He looked at me as to say, "Why are you holding me while this man is doing this to me?"

I also changed many diapers. Sometimes, I wasn't crazy about it, especially when he had a crazy bowel movement. It took a lot for me to do that, but looking back on it now, I had a great time. I am trying to figure out if I was taking care of him or if he was taking care of me. All this time while raising Cory, sometimes the Crohn's Disease would flare up. I remember when he was about 4 or 5 years old, we went to Lancaster, Pennsylvania. That was the only place we could go on vacation with the budget we had at that time. We would go there every year. They had a little 18-hole mini-golf course. That was our favorite activity. I remember going there one day and the next day I got so sick where I was vomiting up. We just got in the car and my wife drove me back to Glen Burnie to the hospital. Then the same routine, stay a week and then come home. Cory was a big help at that age. He could run to the refrigerator and get things for me. Sometimes, I would be so drained and fatigued. I remember taking a shower and had to sit down before I could have enough strength to dry myself off.

My wife was always there with me. Thank God for her. If someone would invite us to come over for dinner or go out with them, I couldn't guarantee them that I'd be able to make it. It worked like this: I could go to take the trash out, then come back in the house and be drained. Or, I'd go outside during the winter and start the car for my wife so it would be warm for her, then come back running in the house and hope no one was in the bathroom.

I was in the hospital during one Easter. I was talking to Sharon on the phone, while she was on her way to church and my teeth were rattling. And I said, "Please hurry up and get down here to me." I remember that someone said that people's teeth rattle. I remember I could not stop shaking and my teeth were rattling. I didn't have false teeth at that time. The nurse came in and gave me some kind of shot to calm me down. That's the effects of Crohn's Disease.

FACES of VALOR

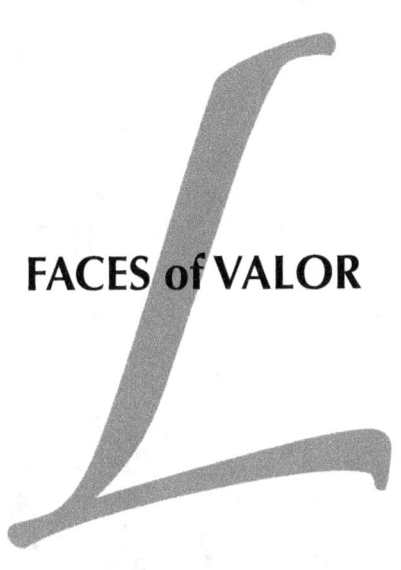

Faces of Valor is a fundraiser to support and honor the men and women in the military, fire, police and EMS services who have been injured in the line of duty as they have protected us and provided safety and security for our American way of life.

Sharon and I attended the event on June 23, 2019, as we had for the last 5 years. This event has been around for 11 years. I thought I could handle it this year watching from the sidelines, but I broke down because I miss riding my bike since losing most of my vision. Just hearing the bikes start up and pulling out sound like sweet music to my ears. Thank God I was still alive and able to attend.

2019 Faces of Valor event

COFFEE TALK WITH LANNIE D.

Why did I write this book? I wrote this book because I thought it would help someone; that is my prayer. For the people that read this book, I do not know what religion, who or what you believe. I believe in Jesus Christ. He is my Lord and Savior and He is the One who got me through all these years of ups and downs, not only with sicknesses, but also with everyday life. When I sit back and think about it, I have been so blessed through all of the troubles. I didn't feel blessed at times, especially when I was going through the toughest of times. The Lord was always there with me, even using the people He put in my life to help me. People like my brother, Larry and Hedy Nelson, who was there for me, Joe and Anna Hall, my wife and my sons. My grandkids have helped me, even when they didn't even know it. When the phone calls came from them, they didn't even realize how timely they were. I also give thanks to the Lord for my church family. Bari, my brother, what can I say? God used you and my brother, Drew, and my sister Gwen, along with so many others – you all were right on time. No one will ever know the depth of how much they helped me. God surely used them with perfect timing, especially when I needed their assistance and when I called on Him; He answered by sending all of them.

It is good when you have friends and family,

and sometimes strangers, they could be angels – for we never know who God may use. I felt so lonely sometimes, especially late in the night when everyone was asleep. The people are gone, and I am awake talking to the Lord, thanking Him for all the people He placed into my life. I know everything was going to be Okay, but I still was nervous at times. Nevertheless, I really was never afraid that I was going to die. I just remember sometimes when my mom or my sister (and other people) would call me on the phone; I would just be a little depressed. They didn't know this when they called, but I would tell them so that they could pray for me. Thus, I know prayer works. So many people were praying for me. I know that's how I got through this journey.

Today, I still having problems with my hands and feet. I do not like the pain, but I look at some people around me that cannot even walk. I can walk and I can talk. I am blind but I can see some, hallelujah. Sometimes, I forget how blessed I am. I still get frustrated, but try not to stay in that mood too long. My friend, Gil, and his wife, Gail Tyler, call me. They are always there for me. Also, Gil is going through a lot of things. Between Gil and Shape (his given name is Delbert Sharps), who is really going through some things, but his attitude is so great it keeps all of us humble. He is paralyzed and has been in a nursing home for over six years. I think his attitude is great and he picks me up when I'm down. He is paralyzed and cannot do anything himself, but he can talk a lot, sometimes talk too much. I'm only kidding (no, I am not --- big smile).

I want to thank the following people for their prayers, encouragement and uplifting words and for being there for me and my family. I couldn't put everyone's name down that was there for me, because I would run out of space.

First of all, I thank my wife, Sharon Dennis, for typing my manuscript for me and being there for all my trials and tribulations. I love her so much. I thank my mother Carrie Dennis, who has always been there for me; everyone that knows her, knows that she is a firecracker. I thank our sons, Troy, Cory and Louis and his wife, Tonya, and my sister, Shirley Ann Holland, for always being there for me; my late brother, James Nick, who always got over on me (smile) – you are truly missed.

I thank our grandkids, Tionna, Troi, Thomas, Taylin, Floyd, Jaylin, Dillon, Devin, Damonte and Dashaun. Ann Marie Holland, my sister-in-laws, Sharlene, Gloria, Jackie, Debbie, Patricia, Peggy and Vlasta; my brother-in-laws, Donald, Carl, Ronald, Danny, and my late brother-in-law, Larry; my cousin, Iva Green. Larry and Hedy Nelson, Gilford and Gail Tyler, George and Gayla Phillips, Orlando and Michelle Phillips, Bari and Karen Azman, the whole Azman family, Low Vision Specialist of Maryland and Virginia, Joseph and Anna Hall, Dorothy and Don Cook, all of my CMA (Christian Motorcyclist Association) and Bayside Believers Chapter members, Barbara and Randy Gray, Jackie Turner, Talicia Blake, Betty Peters, Drew, Marcia and Hanna Shofner, Tom and Marilyn Bell, Cassandra Thomas, Ginger Craig, Gwen Hubbard, George and Julie Yates, Bishop Antonio Palmer and Pastor Barbara Ann Palmer, Delbert Sharps and Sally Jones and Sherry; Raymond (Slick) and Penny Sesker, Deborah Simms, Daniel Nainan, for the private jet flight to New York, it was great. Thank you, Reverend Roberta and Ralph Matthews, Stephen and Edythe Alexander, Governor Larry Hogan and First Lady, Lt. Governor Boyd Rutherford and his wife, the Coffee Talk with Lannie D. crew and followers. Thank you Doretta Jones and Idris Ahmad, for your fervent prayers, everyone at The Church at Severn Run, Pastor Eddie and Sandy Smith, Hope Church, and the late Mrs. Henreitta Sharps, St. Mathews United Methodist Church, Franklin United Methodist church, and Pastor McCauley, Kingdom Celebration Center Family and all the surrounding churches that were praying for me.

Thank you, Kingdom Publishing, LLC and especially Bishop Palmer for guiding me and helping me with my first book, I couldn't have done it without you. Minister Marcello (under Bishop Palmer) for the extra encouragement that pushed me to write this book.

A Note from My Wife

Lannie is usually the stronger person in our family. He makes the final decisions and he plans all of our vacations.

When he was diagnosed with Crohn's Disease, we had to be more aware of our surroundings and where the bathrooms were. We managed and got through that journey.

When he was diagnosed as legally blind, I had to step up and take the reins on driving us around. That wasn't hard. We managed and got through that journey, too.

But when he was diagnosed with cancer, that was a lifestyle change for us all. Until he could get back on his feet, I had to take charge of our home – being responsible for Lannie's medication, feeding tube and wellbeing. Just taking care of him when he got home was an enormous step for me. I consider myself a caregiver by nature, because I am helpful and love to make people comfortable. I was not afraid at all, but just concerned if I was doing the right thing. I was responsible now. Lannie was occasionally moody from the medication or in pain from the surgery. I always told him, "I got your back," which I did, and I love taking care of him. With God's help, we managed to get through this journey and now we are on another one.

A Note from Our Son, Troy

For me, it was very disturbing! When I heard about my father having cancer, so many things started running through my mind. He has been dealing with so many other health issues. Now this! I would think about it all day, every day. For someone who always is going out of his way to help another person, teaching, preaching and just giving words of hope and encouragement, it was hard for me not to ask, "Why him?" But like he dealt with every other illness, he was dealing with this through faith and family. As he got through this test, he showed us again that you never give up on anything and keep on keeping on. It's been a long journey for him and the family, but we know we must stay focused and prepared for the next test.

A Note from Our Son Cory

My dad was placed on full disability in September of 1992. I was born in August of 1992. In short, my dad has been sick my entire life. My childhood consisted of constant trips to the hospital, plans being changed last minute or even cancelled. It made the unpredictability of life even more unpredictable. It was hard, but it was much harder for my dad.

I can't imagine living every day in some sort of pain. But that's what my dad has lived with for decades. As years went on, his vision began to worsen to the point that he is now legally blind. Then, on the last day of July 2018, he was diagnosed with cancer.

I remember hearing the news and thinking, "How much can one man take?" My dad has faced challenge after challenge, health crisis after health crisis and now this?

No person is perfect, and my dad is no exception to this rule. But I can honestly say that my dad has handled these challenges as well as anyone could. He has stayed positive, stayed strong and most importantly kept his faith. I am so proud of my dad for his will to survive and to keep fighting. I hope his strength, faith and love are felt on every page.

Respectfully,
Cory M. Dennis

Some Scriptures that Helped Me

John 8:31-32 (NIV)
31 To the Jews who had believed him, Jesus said, "If you hold to my teaching, you are really my disciples. 32 Then you will know the truth, and the truth will set you free."

John 14:27 (NIV)
27 Peace I leave with you; my peace I give you. I do not give to you as the world gives. Do not let your hearts be troubled and do not be afraid.

John 16:23-24(NIV)
23 In that day you will no longer ask me anything. Very truly I tell you, my Father will give you whatever you ask in my name. 24 Until now you have not

asked for anything in my name. Ask and you will receive, and your joy will be complete.

2 Cor 4:8-9(NIV)
8 We are hard pressed on every side, but not crushed; perplexed, but not in despair; 9 persecuted, but not abandoned; struck down, but not destroyed.

Heb 10:35-36(NIV)
35 So do not throw away your confidence; it will be richly rewarded. 36 You need to persevere so that when you have done the will of God, you will receive what he has promised.

1 Peter 5:7(NIV)
7 Cast all your anxiety on him because he cares for you.

Phil 4:6-7(NIV)
6 Do not be anxious about anything, but in every situation, by prayer and petition, with thanksgiving, present your requests to God. 7 And the peace of God, which transcends all understanding, will guard your hearts and your minds in Christ Jesus.

6 Do not be anxious about anything, but in every situation, by prayer and petition, with thanksgiving, present your requests to God. 7 And the peace

of God, which transcends all understanding, will guard your hearts and your minds in Christ Jesus.

Col 3:15(NIV)
15 Let the peace of Christ rule in your hearts, since as members of one body you were called to peace. And be thankful.

Isaiah 26:3(NIV)
3 You will keep in perfect peace those whose minds are steadfast, because they trust in you.

Psalm 4:8 (NCV)
8 I go to bed and sleep in peace, because, LORD, only you keep me safe.

Mathew 6:25-34 (NCV)
"So I tell you, don't worry about the food or drink you need to live, or about the clothes you need for your body. Life is more than food, and the body is more than clothes. 26 Look at the birds in the air. They don't plant or harvest or store food in barns, but your heavenly Father feeds them. And you know that you are worth much more than the birds. 27 You cannot add any time to your life by worrying about it.
28 "And why do you worry about clothes? Look at how the lilies in the field grow. They don't work

or make clothes for themselves. 29 But I tell you that even Solomon with his riches was not dressed as beautifully as one of these flowers. 30 God clothes the grass in the field, which is alive today, but tomorrow is thrown into the fire. So you can be even more sure that God will clothe you. Don't have so little faith! 31 Don't worry and say, 'What will we eat?' or 'What will we drink?' or 'What will we wear?' 32 The people who don't know God keep trying to get these things, and your Father in heaven knows you need them. 33 Seek first God's kingdom and what God wants. Then all your other needs will be met as well. 34 So don't worry about tomorrow, because tomorrow will have its own worries. Each day has enough trouble of its own.

Prov 3:24 (NIV)
24 When you lie down, you will not be afraid; when you lie down, your sleep will be sweet.

John 8;31-32 (NIV)
31 To the Jews who had believed him, Jesus said, "If you hold to my teaching, you are really my disciples. 32 Then you will know the truth, and the truth will set you free.

John 14:27(NIV)
27 Peace I leave with you; my peace I give you. I do

not give to you as the world gives. Do not let your hearts be troubled and do not be afraid.

John 16:23-24(NIV)
23 In that day you will no longer ask me anything. Very truly I tell you, my Father will give you whatever you ask in my name. 24 Until now you have not asked for anything in my name. Ask and you will receive, and your joy will be complete.

2 Cor.4:8-9(NIV)
8 We are hard pressed on every side, but not crushed; perplexed, but not in despair; 9 persecuted, but not abandoned; struck down, but not destroyed.

Hebrews 10:35-36(NIV)
35 So do not throw away your confidence; it will be richly rewarded. 36 You need to persevere so that when you have done the will of God, you will receive what he has promised.

1 Pet.5:7(NIV)
7 Cast all your anxiety on him because he cares for you.

This is a thank you letter to God that I wrote back in 1989 that I wrote to my parents, as I was dealing with Crohns Disease.

"Thank You God for Your True Love"

First, God, I want to THANK YOU for my mother and father, I did not know how special my mother and father really were. I did not know that God even existed. THANK YOU, GOD for being there when I was so small, running around and stepping on nails in my feet. You were right there helping me, and I did not know you were there. THANK YOU, GOD for when I was raised up on a farm and so many things that I did not realize, like how poor we were moneywise, but how rich we were as a family, THANK YOU.

THANK YOU, GOD for when I was in a three-room house with two families (sometimes three families) living all together and my parents tried to make ends meet and trying to feed us; I was running around and didn't know any better.

THANK YOU, GOD. Oh, I want to THANK YOU, GOD, for when I had scarlet fever and could not walk. My parents (I remember now how concerned they were) – I never had a brand-new bike before, mostly secondhand toys – that day I'll never forget my parents buying me a brand-new bike and I couldn't even walk to it. I remember my father standing there. It never seemed like things worried him, but I saw in his eyes that day, that he was worried; that his son might have Polio or something, and my mother was worried, too. THANK YOU, GOD, because I didn't even know what was going on. I didn't even know that God was there. I didn't even know what it was.

THANK YOU, GOD, for allowing controversies in my life and staying there with me to help me deal with it. THANK YOU, GOD, that when my parents moved into their new house you taught me to be appreciative of running water and an indoor toilet. I realized where I came from.

Oh, THANK YOU, GOD, for a mother who sent me to Sunday school; she made me go when I didn't want to go. Other kids were laughing at me, other kids didn't have to go. THANK YOU, GOD, for giving my mother having the strength to send me there.

THANK YOU, GOD, for the community that I was brought up in, for so many friends and family helping each other out. THANK YOU, GOD, for my brother and sister, I know I got on their nerves sometimes, but they got on mine, too (smile).

The Inspiring Story of Lannie Dennis

THANK YOU, GOD, for letting us all stay as a family. THANK YOU, GOD, for as I grew up and experienced different things and different people, I thought I couldn't find you and all I had to do was open the door. And the door was my heart. THANK YOU, GOD, for having so much patience with me and love for me.

THANK YOU, GOD, for being with me as I went through a painful divorce and the only divorce that I will ever go through. THANK YOU, GOD, for being with me when I was thinking about hurting myself and Satan was there pushing me on. THANK YOU, GOD, fir just reaching it and holding me.

THANK YOU, GOD, for my wife – through you – who brought us together as one (and made me whole). THANK YOU, GOD, for my children. They keep me straight and bring me in, especially Cory. He keeps me straight by asking me, "Why, why?" THANK YOU, GOD, for Louis, a teenager, doing teenager things, and Troy, a man now and doing his own thing. THANK YOU, GOD, for the family that keeps me straight, keeps me balanced and keeps me focused.

THANK YOU, GOD, for the love you give me that I can never return. THANK YOU, GOD, for patience and the time that you let me sit and look out the window and feel the breeze while I'm dealing with the Crohn's disease. THANK YOU,

GOD, for being with me through the operations. THANK YOU, GOD, for just letting me pick up just the tip of the cross, to bear some of my struggles, my sicknesses, racism, trials and tribulations; to show me and to make me a stronger person, THANK YOU, GOD. I love you, THANK YOU for keeping me going, and THANK YOU for your patience and THANK YOU for forgiving me so many times.

Lannie M. Dennis

True love starts with learning to love God. God informs you about self-love. Self-love starts with self-knowledge. Self-knowledge starts with knowing God and your historical roots; where you came from, where you are now, and where you are going.

The Inspiring Story of Lannie Dennis

A Walking Memorial
by Cory Dennis
February 20, 2009
Annapolis Area Christian School
African American Culture Café Night

A memorial, the preservation of a memory of importance. There are many memorials. For example, the Lincoln Memorial, World War II Memorial and others like them. A memorial could be anything, like a monument, a picture, or even a name written on a basketball shoe. Behind every memorial there is a story, a reason why it is there, a reason why it's worth being there. The same can be said for us, behind every person there is a story, a reason why we are here, a reason we do what we do; a walking memorial.

Each person is unique in that we all have our own story; we all have a unique background with different people, places, and events. These instances affect our lives no matter how small. Each person we meet, each sight we see provides an outlook we would not otherwise have had. When we live our lives, we are not simply living them for ourselves, it is more than that, we reflect more than that. As Christians, we are to reflect the love of God in our lives, we reflect our family, we reflect the character of those who have touched our lives who are no longer here.

People say that I have accomplished things that I should be very proud of. I hope these same people don't think that it was simply my doing, because it wasn't. Only through the wonderful grace of God have I been able to do the things that I've done, and through the people that He has placed both in and out of my life. They have affected and touched my life in ways that they will never know. In some ways my life is a memorial to them, I say this because I am who I am because of whom they were and still are. They have taught me much and I strive to put in to practice what I have learned from them, so that when they look down at me, they see what they meant to me. I am a walking memorial.

I am a memorial to those who have touched my life, we all are. We all have been forever changed by a word spoken or a deed done. We all are a reflection of those who have touched our lives. We all have a story to tell, a memory to preserve and we do that by simply living our lives, by simply going to school or going to work, or simply saying thank you. Perhaps the next time someone says, "Thank you," we ought to silently say, "Thank them." I thank them for what they meant to me, I thank them for what they did for me, and I thank them for the time they gave. My life is a memorial to them, they are the reason I stand today, when you see me I can only hope and pray that you see them as well.

To contact the author please visit our website at
www.lannied.com
or email Lannie at
lannie@lannied.com.

PICTURES

STARPOINT SINGING GROUP

INTERVIEW WITH CHANNEL 7

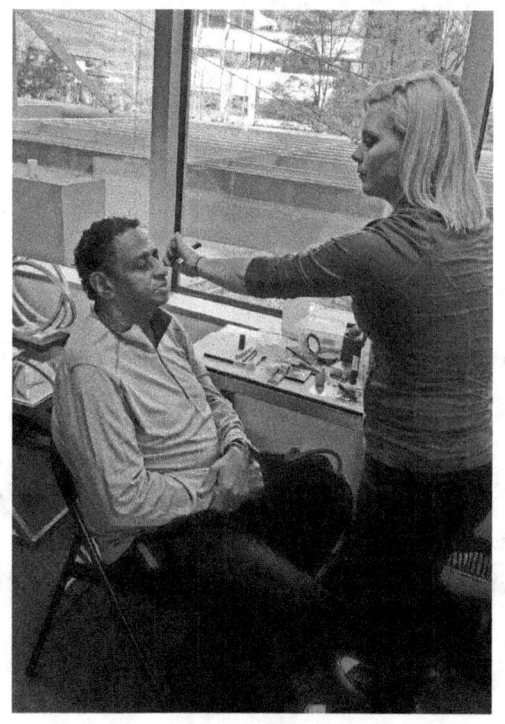

COFFEE TALK WITH LANNIE D

(PRIVATE PLANE RIDE TO NEW YORK)

ME AND GOVERNOR HOGAN IN SUITE AT THE BALTIMORE RAVENS GAME

INTERVIEW AT GOVERNOR HOGAN'S ELECTION

OUR PARENTS AT OUR WEDDING

OUR FAMILY

OUR SON, CORY, GRADUATION FROM UNITED STATES NAVAL ACADEMY

God Is Good

2015

ME AND CORY WITH SHAPE, SALLY AND SHERRY

ME WITH MOM AND SISTER AT MOM'S 95TH BIRTHDAY PARTY

MOM WITH HER GRANDKIDS

PICTURES FROM BELL RINGING CEREMONY

CEERTIFICATE FROM MISSLE DEFENSE AGENCY FOR MY PRESENTATION

My granddaughter, Tionna's painting displayed at the Annapolis Mall.

www.ingramcontent.com/pod-product-compliance
Lightning Source LLC
Chambersburg PA
CBHW052155110526
44591CB00012B/1966